Breaking the Spirit
—— of ——
Religion

by
Pastor Thomas Kato

Breaking the Spirit of Religion
Copyright ©2022 by Thomas Kato

All rights reserved. This book or any portion there of may not be reproduced or used in any manner whatsoever without the express written permission of the publisher except for the use of brief quotations in a book review.

ISBN: 978-0-9971719-2-1

Cover design by:
Alicia Spikes: designsbyrestore@gmail.com

Published by:
Enduring Publishing,
LLC: enduringpublishingllc@gmail.com
773-236-0730

Contents

Foreword v
The Spirit of Religion (Introdcution) 1
Doctrine 3
Denominations 5
Hypocrisy... 7
Legalism and The Pharisees..................................... 9
The Pulpit 11
Religious Control 13
Religious Songs and Sounds 15
Religious Garments 17
Religious Whooping 18
Breaking the Spirit Of Religion 20
Confessions for Breaking the Spirit of Religion 22

Foreword
by
Anthony Briscoe

THERE IS NO DOUBT THAT CHRISTIANITY, BE IT EUROCENTRIC OR westernized in America, has been laced with controversy that has caused a rift within its belief system. Several denominations, styles of delivery in preaching, and varying small non-essential views have led to continual separation within the Body of Christ. It has left a scathing and often stereotypical view of Christianity in the hearts of non-believers.

In Breaking the Spirit of Religion, author Pastor Thomas Kato shares the area of focus where all Christians should be concerned. Sharing, teaching, and preaching the Gospel of Jesus Christ is that centralized focal point. There is no more significant connector for Christians than the Gospel. The death, burial, and resurrection of Jesus, the Christ, is the unifying call for all who believe. To break the spirit of religion, a bold approach to ministry has to confront hypocrisy and ritualism.

Thomas' first work is to raise awareness before he begins to tackle these varying topics in a more detailed, in-depth, and scholarly approach. Be challenged, be enlightened, and most of all, be ready to dialogue with your study groups on how you can begin to Break the Spirit of Religion.

The Spirit of Religion

Introduction

RELIGION IS A PARTICULAR SYSTEM OF FAITH CREATED BY SATAN through the traditions of men to keep believers in captivity and prevent them from experiencing the reality of life in Christ. Religion controls an organized faith which includes the idea of unstructured (confused) people not in the complete formation (pattern) of the Kingdom of God. For example, the Baptist group is distant. There was only one baptist and that was John the Baptist, who (water) baptized Jesus in Matthew 3:13-15. The word baptist is a Greek word pronounced *baptizo* which means to be immersed in water. The second group is the Church of God in Christ which is withdrawn. Jesus said, "Upon this rock I will build my church and the gates of hell shall not prevail against it", Matthew 16:18. The third group is the Methodist which is removed. There is only one method whereby we must be saved, Acts 4:12. The Pentecostal group is solitary. The Day of Pentecost was the release of power from on high that came upon the 120 believers, including the 12 Apostles, which prepared them for the apostolic ministry at best. Pentecost was never designed to become a denomination or a recognized branch of the Christian church with slightly different beliefs within the same faith. It was designed to be a work of the Holy Spirit.

To be religious is to be a person or group of people believing in God or gods and following the practices of that group. This is not parallel to Christ. They have a form of godliness but no power. They will love themselves and money more than God. They will try to hurt those who are good and will abandon friends. They will not receive the grace that is for a Christian. They hold to a form of outwardness (religion) although they have denied the inward work. Their conduct nullifies their claim of faith. Fear is a part of the equation that will fail the hearts of men and their love for Christ will wax cold but our faith in Jesus makes us whole. We have love, power, and a sound mind.

Doctrine

THE TRUE DOCTRINE OF CHRIST IS VERY IMPORTANT TO UNDERstand. They are sets of beliefs taught by a church, such as articles of faith, ideologies, and theories on a position or principle about the Word of God. Doctrine has often been taken out of context to support a certain group of people for the sake and appearance of being right. There has been so much division in the church and a complete separation that has many people confused about the truth. The devil has done a good job of propagating a split in the church that has caused hatred and anger among believers. The scripture says let there be no division among you. Kingdom teaching about Christ is the only way to resolve this level of ignorance. His message will bring healing, deliverance, breakthrough, and knowledge to the body of believers. We are His people and we cannot continue to listen to this jargon that keeps God's people in bondage. Reformation is coming to us and freedom is here. It's a new day and false doctrine must be challenged and put on display so all can know the truth. Greater things are coming for Christ's Church and we are an integral part of this transition. For no one can lay a foundation other than the one which is already laid, that is Jesus Christ. Jesus called the Pharisees hypocrites in Matthew 15:9. He said their worship of Him is worth nothing. They teach what men have made up. 2 John 9 (NIV) states, "Anyone who runs ahead and does not continue in the teaching of Christ does not have God; whoever continues in the teaching has the Father and the Son".

Denominations

DENOMINATIONS ARE RELIGIOUS MOVEMENTS OR BRANCHES THAT have shaped the mentality of Christians for centuries. It is a section of religions, including local churches and groups with distinct explanations of faith in its own organization. Denominations can be traced back to the Protestant Reformation movement to reform the Roman Catholic Church during the 15th century led by Martin Luther, after which the Lutheran church was birthed. There were disagreements over interpretations of scripture which caused a breach in the witness of the church and a great rift was formed. 1 Corinthians 12:12 notes there is one body but different members and Christians have been determined to prove what they believe is right.

Denominations are rooted in the spirit of pride where ungodly men and women have pushed this agenda to sway believers and lock them into one way of serving God. The message of Christ, at large, has been contaminated because of the ignorance that has caused great spiritual carnage within the church. The central focus for all denominations should be about Christ, the

Chief Apostle, and High Priest. Where there is confusion, envy, and strife there is also every evil work. The rules of denominations are very rigid, abrasive, and cause many to backslide into sin. Ultimately, it destroys lives because of stringent requirements, regulations, policies, terms, and conditions by demonized people.

Jesus knew the thoughts of the Pharisees and said unto them, *"Every kingdom divided against itself is brought to desolation, and every city or house divided against itself shall not stand".* We must endeavor to keep the unity of the spirit in the bond of peace. Jesus prayed in John 17:21, *"May they all be as one, Father as you are in me and I am in you. May they belong to us. Then the world will believe that you sent me."*

Hypocrisy

HYPOCRISY IS HUGE IN CHURCHES TODAY. HYPOCRISY IS DEFINED as follows. *1.) The practice of claiming to have moral standards or beliefs to which one's own behavior does not conform. 2.) A person who pretends to have certain attitudes or feelings that are inconsistent with their actions. 3.) Behaviors that are not aligned to righteousness.*[1] It's a false pretense of character or principles which a person doesn't possess. Hypocrites would learn about the Kingdom but never fully walk in the revelation of the Kingdom. In Matthew 23:13, Jesus called the Pharisees hypocrites. They didn't practice what they preached. They wanted to be seen of men and they also wanted respect in the marketplace. When Christ was teaching in the synagogue about humility they failed miserably. They were more concerned about reserved seating. They cleansed the outside of the cup and dish, but inside they were full of greed and selfishness. Like wolves, they devoured widows to make long prayers. Jesus told them that they were full of bones and decaying corpses on the inside, full of hypocrisy and sin, but on the outside

---

1 https://www.merriam-webster.com/dictionary/hypocrisy

they appeared good. 1 Peter 2:16 says, *"Live as those who are free and not as those who use their freedom as a pretext for evil, but live as God's servants".* Titus 1:16 says, *"They claim to know God, but by their actions they deny him".* They are disgusting, disobedient, and disqualified from doing anything good. This spirit will be judged by God himself and will be extracted from the earth. God's repayment is forever!

Legalism and The Pharisees

THE SPIRIT OF RELIGION IS VERY LEGALISTIC TOWARD THE BELIEVER. Legalism is defined as excessive adherence to the law. Legalists have a certain way of thinking with stringent rules that are very critical and judgmental. It puts the Law (Mosaic) before the Gospel. Legalism also puts emphasis on formal structures of religious institutions. It advocates a system of laws that are rigid and prescribe punishments and rewards for unethical behavior. An example is criticism of a person who has to work their job on Sunday but never considers the circumstances or reasons why they have to work. They operate strongly in accusation and abuse the scripture which sounds like the Pharisees. The Pharisees were a group of Jewish members that opposed the Sadducees teaching. The Sadducees didn't believe in the resurrection, life after death, angels or demons; they only believed in the Torah. The Pharisees on the other hand were legal experts who mastered the law. They also believed in the oral law which were laws and legal interpretations that were not recorded in the Five Books of Moses also known as

The Torah. They added 613 additional laws that could not be kept. These laws were strict Jewish traditions and religious practices. The law was a schoolmaster to lead the Jews to Christ. They changed Judaism from a religion of sacrifice to one of keeping the commandments.

Animal sacrifice continued in the Jerusalem temple until it was destroyed by the Romans in 70 AD. Pharisees promoted work over sacrifice. It's a man made tradition that is very contentious, rebellious, deceptive, unforgiving, and breeds false hope. Where the spirit of the Lord is there emancipation from bondage, true liberation. When people do not listen to God's teachings, He does not listen to their prayers. Loving God means obeying his commands. God's commands are not too hard for us. Everyone who is a child of God has the power to win against the world.

Be sure you are not led away by the teaching of those who have nothing worth listening to and only intend to deceive you. This type of teaching is not from Christ. It is only human tradition and comes from the powers that influence this world.

The Pulpit

PULPITS ARE AN ELEVATED PLATFORM OR A READING DESK USED in preaching and conducting worship services. Nehemiah 8:4a lays the foundation for such practice. *"Ezra was standing on a wooden platform that had been built for the occasion".* In verse 5a it states, *"As Ezra stood there on the platform high above the people, they all kept their eyes fixed on him".* Ezra stood where he read the law to Israel who was assembled in Jerusalem. Pulpits are legitimate. In verse 8 it reinforces that the pulpit is where the word of God is read and broken down. It provides understanding, instruction, and allows personal application. When you stand on a platform, the sound echoes throughout the room where everyone can hear the sermon being taught.

Chairs are not suitable on the pulpit. Some churches have 10 to 50 chairs behind the podium and some on the side of the platform, which is dysfunctional. Pulpits are not a place where you sit in chairs and hide. There shouldn't be any chairs in the pulpit at all. Apostles, Pastors, Elders, Bishops, and Leadership should sit on the front row in the congregation with everyone else. Most times preachers chew gum in chairs; they talk too much in chairs; they are asleep in chairs. They sit in chairs and size up the congregation like they are a judge in a court of law; this is out of order. Pulpits are best by themselves so all attention is drawn to the deliverer of the Word and allows congregants to focus solely on the minister.

Religious Control

THERE ARE MANY PEOPLE CONTROLLED BY THE SPIRIT OF RELIGION through ungodly men, especially pastors who are loaded with pride. Control is defined as the power to influence or direct one's behavior or the course of events against their will. Many pastors don't believe in team ministry or liberty. Some pastors believe in a theocracy where Jesus does not rule but they rule the people. They control every aspect of ministry, never letting anyone flourish in their gifts, never promoting or encouraging people, never imparting new levels of grace to their leaders to push them in their gifts. Rather, they stifle them, which paralyzes their growth and prevents forward progression. This spirit is directly connected to pride. Proverbs 16:18, *"Pride goes before destruction, a haughty spirit before a fall".* This spirit works in churches destroying innocent lives because of ignorance. Pastors who control people are very insecure and full of fear. They deal with issues from past encounters that have never been addressed and resolved. This will eventually shipwreck the whole congregation. This can also be considered narcissistic behavior. They are self-centered, arrogant, selfish, demanding, cocky, and need excessive admiration. This is rooted in rejection. They are self-absorbed and very cynical in their approach. The spirit of control will be judged along with those who operate in that spirit. Watch out for those who cause divisions and offenses among you. When they antagonize you by speaking of things that are contrary to the teachings that you've received, don't be caught up in their snare. Deliverance is the children's bread.

Religious Songs and Sounds

RELIGIOUS SONGS AND SOUNDS ARE OLD AND STALE. THEY HAVE no life in them. They stem from the time of slavery. Those old Negro songs, anthems, hymns, and sounds brought the slaves through because that's all they knew and they held on for life. Songs that resemble this old way have been based on tradition. If I start singing any of the following songs I'm sure you could finish each of them. For instance, *"Pass me not oh gentle savior…, I'm on the battlefield for my Lord, One glad morning when this life is over I'll fly away, Do not pass me by, Won't he make me clean inside, It's alright now believe I'll make it anyhow, Lead me; guide me along the way."*

As time progressed the church began to embrace those songs and sounds. There has been an imprint within the structure of the musical aggregation of the church that for many has not changed. We remember where we come from and where it all began, but it's a new day. We must sing unto the Lord a new song. We cannot put the Father in an old vase and expect new flowers to manifest. Oil and water don't mix. Greens and mayonnaise don't mix. Oatmeal and hot sauce don't mix. You get the point!

Our songs should be led by the spirit of God. Some rehearsed songs are good but that shouldn't be the thrust of our drive to bring in God's glory. Anointed songs bring God's manifest presence. He will dwell among us. He will sup with us and that's what we want. We want spontaneous songs prompted by the Holy Ghost. They must be new and fresh. They set the atmosphere for miracles. They open the heavens. New sounds can produce God's might in a service. As referenced in I Chronicles 14:15, in sounds of war God will strike his enemies.

New sounds open the heavens and cause breakthroughs in our midst. Our songs and sounds must be current for the time in which we live. This is what we want. We must assimilate and acclimate to new dimensions of glory and power in worship.

Religious Garments

Many preachers dress in various types of religious garments such as clergy collars and robes. These robes and collars are like quilts and linen that you get from the house. This is trending in denomination circles. Men look holy but their lives are raggedy. Looking holy does not make you anointed. Looking up to par does not make you spiritual. Walking in power as Jesus did makes you anointed. Performing miracles makes you anointed. Casting out demons makes you anointed. Healing the sick makes you anointed. Living clean makes you holy. I will not wear any religious garments, attire, costumes, regalia, outfits, apparel, trappings, raiments, uniforms, etc. It's not what you wear but what's in your heart. The pure in heart shall see God. Your outward man perishes but your inward man is being renewed day by day. It's not your attire but your obedience to the father. If you're willing and obedient, you will eat the good of the land. It's not what you put on but what you pull off. Those who are Christ's have crucified the flesh with its passions and desires.

Religious Whooping

WHOOPING IS A FORM OF PREACHING THAT IS ROOTED IN RELI-gion. It's an old way of proclaiming the Word of God. They try to exegete the scripture for 15 minutes then whoop, scream and moan for 45 minutes. This is fleshly motivated, to say the least. There is no power in this kind of expression. In my estimation, we already had praise and worship in the service, why do we need moaning from the preacher? Many preachers are stuck in an old pattern of exciting the appetites of carnal people because they themselves are carnal by whooping. They change five instrument keys on the keyboard and spit tobacco juice on people and call that preaching. They make statements like, won't he do it, ain't he alright, hold my mule, I'm like Daniel in the lion's den, he's sweet I know, can I get a witness, y'all ain't saying nothing, shake somebody's hand and say neighbor, is there anybody here that knows God is still on the throne, he'll step right in on time, shout yea, hug your neighbor then shake'em and rock'em, he'll turn it around, have I got a witness, joy will come in the morning, early Sunday morning he got up out of the grave with all power, yes he will, by Pastor Thomas Kato

I'm still on the wall, he still working it out, do I have a witness, lift your holy hands, everything is gonna be alright, say neighbor I don't know about you, if it had not been for he Lord on my side, where would I be, I've seen the lightning flashing, I seen the thunder rolling, I've seen the breakers dashing, be still and know the I am God, fight on, Jacob won't lose his reward, say yea, uh uh uh uh uh uh uh uh uh uh. They sound like they have a frog in their throat; it sounds like they are gasping for breath with asthma and bronchitis. It sounds like a diesel engine running in their windpipe. It is religion and tradition on steroids. It is carnal, sensual, worldly, and fueled by fleshly passions to get people's emotions stirred up rather than wanting to see genuine change. It does not bring spiritual growth. It brings stagnation to the believer. Jesus taught in the synagogue; he did not squall.

Breaking the Spirit Of Religion

SUPERNATURAL INTELLIGENCE, KNOWLEDGE, UNDERSTANDING, and revelation will be released as you delve into this publication. Religion is a spirit that has gripped the life of the church for centuries and has caused great calamity in the lives of precious people that ultimately brought them to their spiritual demise. This spirit operates either from the soul realm or the flesh. It's rooted in rituals, church practices, and customs. It promotes pride and arrogance. It causes division and strife. It pushes ignorance and deception. We have the power, through Christ, to break the spirit of religion, and here are a few ways. 1) We must bind this spirit through prayer. He will not allow anything you don't allow. When we speak of God's judgment on earth it will be God's judgment. 2) In prayer, we loose freedom in Christ; who the Son sets free is free indeed. 3) We follow the Spirit. We get our new life from the Spirit so we should follow the spirit. 4) We must study the Word of God and grow in the grace and knowledge of our Lord and Savior Jesus Christ. 5) We must be faithful to his Word. For the Word of the Lord is upright, and all his work is done in faithfulness. *Psalm 119:105* (AMPC), "Your word is a lamp to my feet and a light to my path." *Psalm 119:11* (ESV), "I have stored up your word in my heart that I might not sin against you." 6) Get the demon spirit of religion cast out of you. He also wants us to have the power to force demons out of people. 7) Lastly, have faith in the Heavenly Father; the just shall live by faith. These are tools that will help believers break and eradicate the spirit of religion.

Confessions for Breaking the Spirit of Religion

HEAVENLY FATHER, I THANK YOU THAT I AM NO LONGER BOUND by the yoke of religion, but I am free through the blood of Christ. Today I confess that wisdom, knowledge, and understanding come upon me, and I will walk in liberty, for I seek your precepts. Establish my footsteps in your word, and do not let any wrongdoing have dominion over me. I will read and study your word only and be led by the Holy Spirit.

Father, I thank you that I will not be controlled by demonized pastors, ministers, or leaders. I am a son of God and I'm led by the Spirit of God. I will not succumb to foolish antics but will seek the truth of God's word. Your word is a lamp unto my feet, and a light unto my path. Your word is like a hammer that breaks into pieces. I will pray, fast, and consecrate to maintain my status in Jesus. As Christ was clean, I am also a clean vessel used by God.

I refuse to be ignorant and accept false doctrine or false teachings. I will know the truth, and the truth will set me free. Whom the son (Christ) sets free, is free indeed. I will study to show myself approved. I will rightly divide the word of truth.

Lord, I thank you that you will teach me what to say, so I will know how to encourage people. Morning after morning, I will listen for your direction. Uncover my eyes, so that I may see miraculous things in your teachings.

Heavenly Father, from this day forward, I purpose, to follow your commands and a stranger I will not follow. Let me hear your voice and I will obey only you.

www.ingramcontent.com/pod-product-compliance
Lightning Source LLC
Chambersburg PA
CBHW070739020526
44118CB00035B/1774